know your pet

AQUARIUM FISH

Joan Palmer

The Bookwright Press
New York · 1989

Know Your Pet

Cats   Rabbits
Dogs   Hamsters

First published in the
United States in 1988 by
The Bookwright Press
387 Park Avenue South
New York, NY 10016

First published in 1988 by
Wayland (Publishers) Limited,
61 Western Road, Hove,
East Sussex, BN3 1JD, England.

Library of Congress Cataloging-in-Publication Data

Palmer, Joan
    Aquarium fish/by Joan Palmer
        p.   cm. — (Know your pet series)
    Includes index.
    Summary: Gives instructions for setting up and
maintaining an aquarium and for caring and feeding
the fish that will make it their home. Also discusses
the history of fish as pets and their relationship to
people.
    ISBN 0-531-18250-9
    1. Aquarium fishes — Juvenile literature.
    2. Aquariums — Juvenile literature. [1. Aquarium
fishes. 2. Aquariums.] I. Title. II. Series.
SF457.25.P35   1989
639.3'4—dc 19   88–7263
                                              CIP
                                               AC

Designed and produced by BLA Publishing
Limited, East Grinstead, Sussex, England.

A member of the Ling Kee Group
LONDON · HONG KONG · TAIPEI · SINGAPORE · NEW YORK

Photographic credits

t = top, b = bottom, l = left, r = right

cover: Trevor Hill

8, 9t, 9b Trevor Hill; 10 Geological Museum; 11
Orion/NHPA; 14, 15, 18, 19, 20, 21, 24, 25t, 25b, 26t,
26b, 27, 28t, 28b, 30, 32t, 32b, 33, 34, 35, 36, 37t
Trevor Hill; 37b G.I. Bernard/NHPA; 38, 40, 41, 42,
43t, 43b Trevor Hill

Editorial planning by Jollands Editions
Color origination by Waterden Reproductions
Illustrations by Mick Loates/Linden Artists; and
David Webb/Linden Artists
Printed in Italy by G. Canale & C.S.p.A. – Turin

Cover: **The Emperor Angel, with its
bright blue and yellow stripes and
yellow fins, is a popular aquarium
fish. It is very hardy, but can be
aggressive toward other large
species of Angelfish.**

**Title page: The Texas Cichlid is almost 5 cm
(2 in) long when fully grown.
Although somewhat aggressive
and fond of uprooting plants, it is
a very beautiful fish. It is the only
Cichlid that is native to the United
States.**

Contents

Note to the Reader

In this book there are some words in the text that are printed in **bold** type. This shows that the word is listed in the glossary on page 44. The glossary gives a brief explanation of words that may be new to you.

Introduction

Fish make excellent pets. They are beautiful, fun to watch and they take up little of their owner's time. It costs very little to feed them, and the equipment need not be expensive. It is not surprising that the common goldfish, which can live for twenty years or more in an aquarium, is the world's most popular pet. One in ten homes in the United States, Canada and Australia either owns a fish tank or has a goldfish pond in the garden.

An inexpensive hobby

Having an aquarium is fun. It is the perfect hobby because it costs as little — or as much — as you can afford. You can start the hobby with just a couple of fish, but you will soon find yourself becoming more and more interested.

You can leave the fish at home when you go away on vacation if you make a few simple arrangements. You can, if you wish to, join a local aquarium (fishkeepers) society. This is a

▼ People of all ages enjoy having fish at home. A good way to start is to buy a few goldfish. They are fun to watch and easy to keep.

▲ When you get the chance, you should visit a large aquarium shop. It is like going to a small zoo. You will be able to see hundreds of different varieties of fish. Some are quite cheap to buy, others are expensive.

▼ Watching the fish swimming around in an aquarium is said to be good for you. It makes you feel relaxed and peaceful. That is why many dentists and doctors keep a tropical fish tank in their waiting rooms. It keeps people from worrying while they are waiting to be seen.

kind of club where you would meet other **aquarists** and learn about exhibiting your fish at shows. But many people just like to enjoy the quiet pleasure of looking after fish and admiring them.

Watching fish

Watching aquarium fish is good for you! Science has proved it. That is why so many dentists and doctors have tanks of fish in their waiting rooms. Most people are nervous when they visit the dentist. They are afraid of being hurt. Some years ago a scientist studied patients as they watched an aquarium in a dentist's waiting room. These people were found to be less nervous than those who only had books to read or posters to look at. Watching a tank of fish helps you to relax and makes you feel calm.

An aquarium decorates a room and takes up very little space. It creates neither mess nor noise, and adds color and interest to your home, so this is a hobby all the family can enjoy.

Fish and their origins

The forms of life we know today have come about through **evolution**, a word of Latin origin, which means to unfold. Evolution is the way living things gradually changed over millions of years in order to survive.

Billions of years ago, when the earth was very young, most of it was covered by oceans. There was no animal life on land, but the oceans were teeming with minute living things such as tiny plants that were able to move. Then, about 430 million years ago, the first fish appeared in the seas. Some of these had jaws, while others developed into eel-like animals without jaws. The jawed fish divided into two groups, fish with hard bones and others, which later became sharks and rays, with bones made of a softer material.

The sign of the fish

Fish have always provided human beings with food. Ancient drawings and carvings tell us that fish played an important part in human life and beliefs. In **astrology**, Pisces, the Latin word for fish, is one of the twelve signs of the Zodiac. It is always shown as two fish swimming in opposite directions.

▲ The zodiac is the imaginary path in the sky along which the sun and the moon appear to move. The early astronomers divided the zodiac into twelve equal parts, naming each part after a group of stars seen in that part. The ancient sign of Pisces, the two fishes, is the twelfth sign of the zodiac and operates each year between February 19 and March 20.

▼ About 350 million years ago, before the time of the dinosaurs, the shallow seas were teaming with life. There were some varieties of fish with fins and backbones. From these first bony fish there developed the endless varieties of fish that we find today.

► For hundreds of years the Japanese have bred freshwater fish in their garden ponds. These fish include carp and goldfish, but their favourite is Koi, of which there are numerous colorful varieties. Koi can grow to a size of 100 cm (40 in) and the rare varieties are extremely valuable.

Some Japanese gods took the form of fish. The carp was chosen for its power to withstand opposition and to swim against the flow of the stream. It became the symbol of the *Samurai*, a class of Japanese noblemen.

The sign of the fish can still be seen in the early Christian burial tombs beneath Rome. Ichthus is the Greek word for fish, the letters standing for Jesus Christ, Son of God, Savior, from which the early symbol of Christianity, the fish sign, had its origin.

The Chinese and their goldfish

The earliest reports of keeping goldfish in ponds was in China in 1655. The Chinese learned how to develop different varieties of goldfish. They began keeping their fish in china bowls, and so could only view the goldfish from above. So they bred and developed a goldfish that gazes upward toward the sky.

Facts about fish

Fish have bony skeletons inside their bodies.
Like birds and **mammals**, they are called
vertebrates, and have backbones and brains.
But unlike birds and mammals, they do not
breathe air to get **oxygen**. Instead, they draw
in water through their mouths, and take oxygen
from the water as it passes through their **gills**.

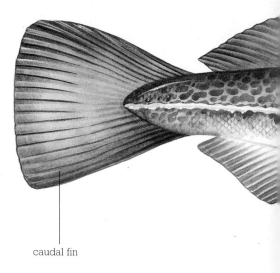

Fins for swimming

You will enjoy watching the fish as they swim
around in your aquarium. Most fish are
covered with small **scales**, and they have **fins**
sticking out from their bodies. The tail moves
from side to side and pushes the fish forward.
The tail is an almost solid mass of muscle.

caudal fin

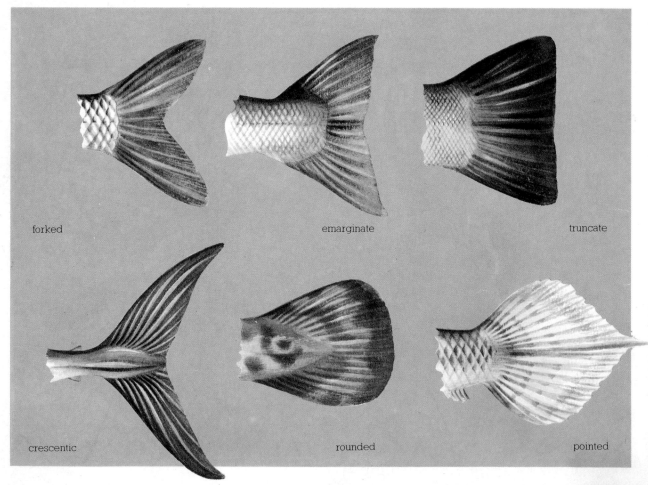

forked

emarginate

truncate

crescentic

rounded

pointed

12

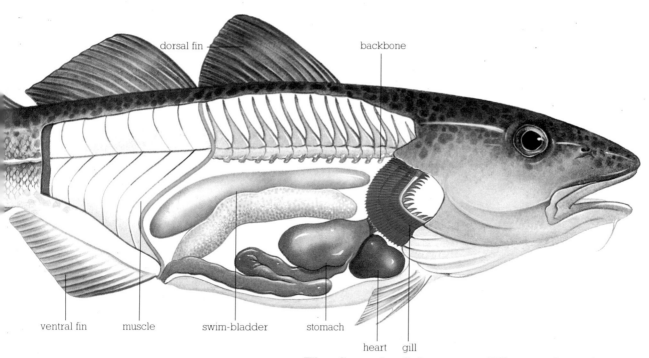

dorsal fin · · · · · · · · · · · · · · backbone

ventral fin   muscle   swim-bladder   stomach

heart   gill

▲ All fish are adapted for life in water. The body is a mass of muscles that are used for movement in the water. Beneath the backbone, some fish have a swimbladder. This helps the fish to stay at a certain depth. The gills are used for breathing.

The fins of a fish serve different functions. The single fins, called **dorsal** on the back and **ventral** on the belly of the fish, act as keels to keep it on its course. The tail, or **caudal**, fin is used for driving the fish forward. The other fins are in pairs, and it is interesting to watch these as they control direction of movement and balance: the **pectoral** fins are the breast fins and are used for quick turning. A stroke of the right side pectoral results in the fish making a smart left turn. The shape and size of the fins vary from one fish to another but they all have their purpose.

Different types of fish

◄ The shape and size of the fins vary from one fish to another, but they all have their purpose. The caudal, or tail fin, is used to drive the fish forward, and there are six basic shapes. Watch your fish carefully as they glide and dart through the water. You will learn how fish use their fins for every kind of movement.

There are over 22,000 different **species** of fish, including some real oddities. The Electric Torpedo Ray can stun its enemies with an electric shock. The armored fish has its head and body encased in a bony box, like the shell of a tortoise. You may not wish to keep fish like these in your home because they are rather large.

Types of aquariums

Before making a start with your new hobby, you must decide what kind of fish you want. Whatever type you choose, you must make sure that your fish live in the right temperature and water conditions.

There are coldwater fish, such as Goldfish and Sticklebacks. These live in fresh water. There are also the colorful tropical fish that come from warm freshwater lakes and rivers of South America, Africa, Asia and Australia.

Marine fish are not so easy to care for. You have to keep the water salty all the time, to match sea water. But you can read about keeping marine fish in this book. Some day you may decide to have a marine tank.

◄ Beginners often start with a coldwater tank, since the water does not need to be heated. As can be seen in the picture, water can soon become discolored and dirty. Your fish must have water of good quality if they are to remain healthy. Frequent water changes and the use of a filter are very important.

The coldwater tank

Goldfish, which are coldwater fish, are not as clean as some fish, and they tend to dirty the water. In order to avoid changing the water each day, you should put a **filter** on your tank. The filter will help to clear the water and keep it pure.

As well as a filter, you will need some washed gravel for the base and a few plastic, or live, **aquatic** plants. You can buy all these things from the pet shop.

▶ It is not always easy to find a good position for your aquarium. This tropical tank is on a firm metal stand and is away from direct sunlight. The electrical wires and connections are out of the way behind the tank. This is good for reasons of safety.

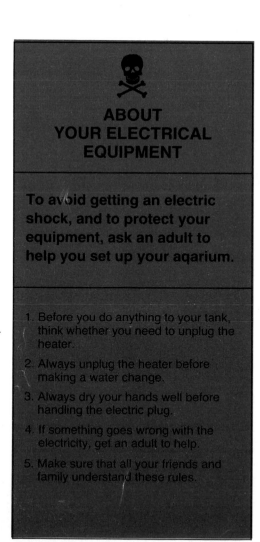

ABOUT YOUR ELECTRICAL EQUIPMENT

To avoid getting an electric shock, and to protect your equipment, ask an adult to help you set up your aqarium.

1. Before you do anything to your tank, think whether you need to unplug the heater.
2. Always unplug the heater before making a water change.
3. Always dry your hands well before handling the electric plug.
4. If something goes wrong with the electricity, get an adult to help.
5. Make sure that all your friends and family understand these rules.

The tropical tank

For tropical fish you should buy a tank with a top cover. The cover helps to reduce **evaporation** from the warm water. It also prevents the fish from jumping out. You will also need an electric heater to heat the water. The **thermostat** will keep it at the right temperature.

A light mounted in the lid of your tank will help you to see your fish better. Although electric lighting adds to the cost of upkeep, it takes the place of sunlight, which fish and plants are normally used to.

Warning

Whether you decide on coldwater or on tropical fish, you will be using electricity. You must ask your parents to help you choose the electrical equipment from the pet shop. You will need their help in fitting the equipment and showing you how to use it.

15

Coldwater fish — Goldfish

Goldfish kept in bowls often die from lack of oxygen. A globe-shaped bowl should only be partly full, with the water up to the wide part of the bowl. That is because oxygen enters the water through the surface. The larger the surface area is, the more oxygen there is in the water.

Plants add oxygen to water. They also give your fish food, shade and shelter. You should never place your tank or bowl near a fire or radiator — nor in direct sunlight.

You can keep certain breeds of goldfish in a garden pond. The fish will survive, even under ice in winter, and will grow in size in this natural **environment**. The pond should have suitable plants in it, some floating and some beneath the surface. The pond should not be near trees since fallen leaves can rot and dirty the water. It may be wise to put wire netting over the pond, so as to protect your fish from cats and from birds that eat fish.

Celestial

Varieties of goldfish

While the Common Goldfish thrives in the garden pond, fancy varieties fare much better indoors. There are over 100 varieties of goldfish, with different tails, bodies and color patterns. They all descend from the Gibel Carp, or Wild Goldfish, which was kept by the Chinese for food 1,000 years ago.

Not all goldfish are gold. The Telescopic-eyed Moor is a black fish with protruding eyes. The Oranda, with a head covered with bumps, is usually orange, and rather clumsy in appearance.

Many varieties have beautiful fins and tails. The Fantail has an **ovoid**, or egg-shaped, body with a double tail. Veiltails have fins and tails that are large and flowing.

▶ Goldfish are the easiest of all fish to keep. You can keep them in a bowl or in an aquarium. Some species can be kept in an outdoor pond. There are numerous varieties of goldfish with different tails, bodies and patterns of color.

Common Goldfish

Comet

Veiltail

Moor

Keeping coldwater fish

The most common fish for a coldwater tank is the Goldfish. But small Koi will take to aquarium life too. Catfish and algae-eating catfish are other popular coldwater varieties.

Lighting and filters

You will find that there are many different types and sizes of tanks available in pet shops. As a beginner, you would be wise to start with a small tank as described on page 20. Later, when you get to know more about fish, you might buy a larger aquarium.

A light mounted in the lid of your tank helps you to see the fish better. If you have live plants in your tank, they need eight or ten hours of light every day.

Your tank may be fitted out with an **air pump** and filter. The filter clears the waste matter from your tank and keeps the water clean. The air pump also produces bubbles and keeps the water moving in the tank. You should ask your parents to help you choose your lighting and filtering equipment from the pet shop. Do not try to set up the electrical equipment yourself. That must be done by an adult who knows about electricity, and can tell you how to use it safely.

▲ The Goldfish, Red Cap and Shubunkins shown in this coldwater tank are popular varieties for the beginner. They will not need any extra heat.

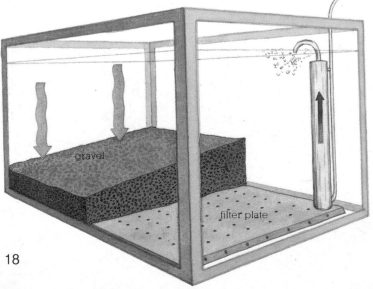

air supply

gravel

filter plate

◄ There are several different types of filtesr. In one kind, a filter plate is placed under gravel where it cannot be seen. Thousands of tiny bacteria live in the gravel. They convert the poisons in the water to less harmful material as a natural process. The aquarium water is continually drawn through the gravel by the action of an air pump. This adds to the oxygen in the water. Without oxygen, the bacteria cannot do their work and will die.

Choosing your fish

To start with, buy just two or three fish. You can build up your stock slowly. The pet shop will put your fish in a small plastic bag or in a plastic carton.

Do not bring your first fish home from the pet shop until your tank has been set up with water for a few days. Do not try to move the tank with water in it. Water is heavy, and the tank might break!

Do not put your fish into the tank right away. Let the air get to the fish by carefully opening the bag while it floats. Then let a little aquarium water into the bag so that the fish may become used to the new water and its temperature before swimming free.

▲ Take plenty of time in choosing your fish. The assistant will net the fish you choose, and place them in a plastic bag for taking back to your home. These will be young fish. Find out what size they will grow to.

19

A tank for the beginner

Some beginners start right off with a large tank, but they can be quite expensive. Most will probably begin with a ten-gallon tank. The tank in the picture is a smaller beginner's tank of a kind that is used mostly in Britain. It is made of strong plastic, and the heater and the air pump are hidden from view behind a false back in the aquarium.

The beginner's tank

The most common tank used in the United States is probably the ten-gallon tank which measures about 50 cm (20 in) long, 30 cm (12 in) wide, and 25 cm (10 in) high. An electric air pump keeps the water moving through a filter and a heater with a thermostat regulates the water temperature.

All you need to do once the tank is working is to rinse out the filter every so often and to change part of the water. How often you do this depends on the kind of pump and filter you buy, so be sure to get clear instructions from the pet shop when you buy your equipment.

◄ **The tank shown in the picture is one of the smallest tanks available. With the lid raised, you can see the hidden compartment at the back of the tank where the heater and the filter tubing are kept. The pump is fixed to the rear of the tank.**

Setting up the tank

When you bring your new tank home, you must find a good place for it. It will need to be close to an electrical outlet, but away from radiators and direct sunlight. A good place would be the corner of a room, where no one will knock into it. It should be placed on a firm table or stand.

First, give the tank a thorough cleaning, but do not use cleaning liquids. Place washed gravel to a depth of about 5 cm (2 in) on the floor of the tank. (You can buy gravel from the pet shop.) Slope the gravel up slightly toward the back. Pour tapwater into the tank very gently, and set the thermostat at the required temperature. You may add some small plants at this stage, and a few rocks and caves for your fish. Now leave the tank for a few days so that the water can settle before you begin adding your fish.

▼ Because of its very small size, this tank will only take a few fish. It is very important not to overstock your tank. As a beginner, you may find it very tempting to buy more fish than your tank will safely hold.

Keeping tropical fish

Tropical fish come from the freshwater lakes and rivers in the **tropics**, near the equator. In these parts the water is normally at a temperature of about 25°C (78°F). If you decide to keep tropical fish, the water in your tank must be kept at about this temperature with a thermostatically controlled heater.

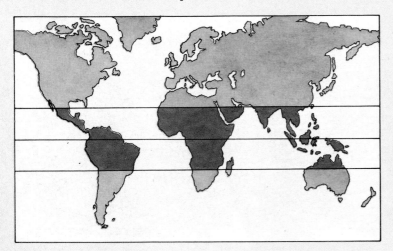

Make sure to unplug the heater and wait ten minutes before taking the heater out of the tank for any reason. (This is so the change of temperature won't crack the heater.) When making water changes you do not need to remove the heater, but be sure to unplug it because the thermostat may be somewhat exposed when you remove part of the water. For safety reasons, always get an adult to help you install and adjust the electrical equipment in your tank.

How many fish can I keep?

It is very important not to overstock your tank with fish. The number of fish you can keep depends more on the surface area of the tank than on its depth. Of course it also depends on the size and length of the fish you decide to keep. The body length of a fish is measured

▶ The tropical fish illustrated on these pages are very popular with fishkeepers. The appearance of many varieties helps you to remember their names. Apart from the Guppy, there are clues to the names of all the varieties illustrated. The Leopard Corydoras is one of the catfish. Catfish have whiskers called barbels. Like cats, many of them are active at night. The Neon Tetras have bright bands of color along the sides of their bodies like neon lights.

◀ All tropical fish come from the lakes and rivers in that part of the world known as the tropics. The tropics lie either side of the equator, and in these parts the sun shines strongly overhead in the middle of the day. The water temperature is usually about 25°C (78°F).

Zebra Danio

Neon Tetra

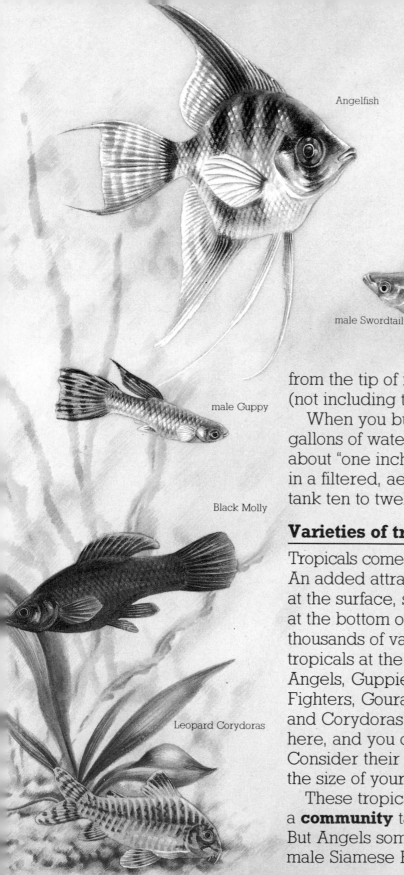

Angelfish

male Swordtail

male Guppy

Black Molly

Leopard Corydoras

from the tip of its snout to the end of the body (not including the tail).

When you buy your tank, ask how many gallons of water it will hold. You can keep about "one inch of fish" for each gallon of water in a filtered, aerated aquarium. In a ten-gallon tank ten to twelve fish is a good number.

Varieties of tropical fish

Tropicals come in all shapes, sizes and colors. An added attraction is that some varieties feed at the surface, some in the middle and others at the bottom of the aquarium. There are thousands of varieties! The ten most popular tropicals at the present time are Neon Tetras, Angels, Guppies, Platies, Swordtails, Siamese Fighters, Gouramies, Mollies, Zebra Danios and Corydoras Catfish. They are illustrated here, and you can study them in pet shops. Consider their body lengths compared with the size of your tank.

These tropical favorites can live together in a **community** tank because they do not fight. But Angels sometimes eat smaller fish and the male Siamese Fighter is not a good choice.

23

Varieties for the specialist

There are so many varieties of tropical fish that it is not easy deciding what fish to keep. As a beginner with a small tank, your best plan would be to keep a selection of small community fish. Later on, you could become a specialist, concentrating on one or more particular species.

◄ These Angelfish appear to be smiling at the photographer with their large eyes. Because of their size, they are best kept in a large, deep tank. They are peaceful fish and are able to mix easily with most other species. Viewed "head-on," the Angelfish is very slender, and thus not easily seen by enemies.

Angelfish

Angelfish are popular fish with the beginner. They belong to the Cichlid family and come mostly from the Amazon. Small Angelfish can be kept in the community tank for a time. But they are **carnivorous** and will eat baby fish. As they grow in size they are best kept with their own species or with larger varieties. Angelfish can grow to 15 cm (6 in) and need a large tank.

There are many varieties of Angelfish and they are beautiful to watch. They are intelligent and can show their feelings. They get to know, and even seem to like, the person who feeds them. They are good parents and often protect their eggs and fry for the first few weeks. They lay their eggs on the sides of leaves or other flat surfaces, such as a piece of slate or a tall flower pot.

Catfish varieties

Corydoras Catfish with their "whiskers," or **barbels**, are fascinating fish. Most of the varieties are quite small, around 5 cm (2 in), and are useful in the community tank. You can rely on them to eat up food that has been lodged in the gravel on the floor of the tank.

There are numerous varieties of catfish. Look for the Glass Catfish. Its flesh is crystal clear and you can see the bones. It looks just like a living skeleton! The Emerald Catfish is very peaceful. The Bronze Catfish spends much of its time testing the bottom of the tank with its barbels. It may, however, cause problems by uprooting plants.

Then there is the Upside Down Catfish. By swimming upside down it feeds on the **algae** beneath the leaves of plants. The Leopard, which is spotted, likes to live on the bottom of the tank.

▲ ▼ The Upside-down Catfish (above) feeds in a belly-up position on the under side of leaves and rocks.

In the picture below, it is not easy to count how many Glass Catfish there are in the shoal. These fish have a pair of long barbels on the upper jaw.

How fish behave

One of the great joys of keeping a well-stocked tank is the interest you get just watching the fish and seeing how they behave. If you are building up a community tank containing different varieties of fish, you will hope that they are all going to get along together. By watching how they behave you will be able to spot the likely trouble-makers.

A fish and its senses

Are fish intelligent? The answer is that fish have senses, as do all animals, and these are adapted to the environment in which they exist. To give an example, some experiments have been carried out with goldfish. A tank was divided by means of a partition. Goldfish were trained to pass through a small hatch when a light flashed so as to receive a food reward. Other goldfish watched what happened and soon learned the trick.

Some fish find their food by means of smell, others by sight and by feel. Fish that hunt by sight usually have large eyes. Some deep-sea fish have the largest eyes of all. But fish that live in caves and have to hunt for their food in the dark may have no working eyes at all. Some of them, however, have feelers or barbels to help them find their food.

In most fish, you can see a line running along each side of the body from head to tail. This is known as the **lateral line**. Along this line there are thousands of tiny nerves that sense movements and pressures in the water. This line helps fish to avoid objects, even in the dark.

Sense of smell varies from one type of fish to another. In some, like the shark, the sense is strong and it can smell blood. Other fish rely more on eyesight.

▲ Even in the safety of the aquarium, fish often swim around together in a shcool. That is one way in which smaller fish can protect themselves against attack by larger fish.

▼ On many fish, including the one in this picture, you can see a line that runs along the side of the body. It is called the lateral line. Beneath it there are thousands of little nerve ends. These help the fish to sense any changes of pressure in the water.

How fish behave

Fish do not sleep the way we do. They rest by keeping quite still, as though day-dreaming. You can sometimes see them in this state.

Watch your fish as they move around together. Swimming together in a school, is their way of protecting themselves against attack. Watch what happens when you put a new fish into your tank. It will soon join up with its fellows.

▼ If carefully selected, several different species of fish can live together peacefully in the community tank. Some, like the Platies and the Swordtail seen in the picture, spend most of their time near the top of the tank. Others are happier near the bottom of the tank.

Plants for your aquarium

There are many reasons why you should have plants in your aquarium. In daylight, or when the tank is lit, plants take in a gas called **carbon dioxide** and give off oxygen. In fish, the process works the other way 'round. So plants help in a small way to clean the water of waste and provide balance.

Of greater importance, plants provide a refuge and territories for each of your fish. You can watch fish in their tanks in the pet shop as they lurk and hide near plants. Sometimes you may have to wait quite some time for a hiding fish to come out from its shelter. Plants provide some food for fish that are vegetarians, and also safe breeding areas. Above all, they add to the beauty of an aquarium, and give your tank a natural appearance.

◄ ▲ **Here are two examples of good natural environments for tropical fish. In the lower picture, small fish can use the log as a natural refuge and hiding place from possible enemies.**

Types of plants

You may decide to have only plastic plants as decoration and to provide cover for your fish. They are of course easier, but not nearly so natural. It is important to seek advice from the pet shop when buying live plants. There are floating plants, low-growing plants and high-growing plants.

There are numerous species of plants, and two popular ones are Anacharis and Ludwigia. They are strong and will thrive in coldwater or tropical tanks. These plants root well from cuttings, which can be easily obtained.

Plants with leaves that float freely include the Underwater Banana Plant, which has banana-like roots that "sit" on the gravel. The Water Sprite has dangling roots, which make a good hiding place for young **fry**, and there is also the Java Moss.

The pet shop will give you advice about planting these, and about other quick-growing varieties. When you bring your plants home, draw a plan of how you are going to arrange them. Put the low-growers in the front or sides and the high-growers at the back of the tank. Push the plant roots gently into the gravel, and anchor them with small weights or pebbles if you need to. Better still, give them a good rooting base, such as peat moss pots, which are sold in aquarium shops.

▼ The plants shown here are easy to grow in the tropical tank. Your local aquarium shop will be able to show you many others.

Duckweed

Salvinia

Vallisneria

Acorus

Amazon Sword Plant

Aponogeton

29

Feeding your fish

In the oceans, fish live and feed at various levels, according to species. In your tank, the same sort of thing happens, and each variety prefers to feed at its chosen depth. Some fish will feed on the bottom of the tank, like most of the Catfish for instance. Swordtails will eat at the surface, and the colorful little Neon Tetras in the middle of the tank.

In an aquarium, many more fish die of overfeeding than of starvation. "Little and often" is the rule with fish-feeding. Sprinkle just a pinch of flakes on the surface of your tank. If the food is eaten within a minute or two and the fish seem to be looking for more, add another pinch. Be careful not to forget the Catfish or other bottom-feeders. Usually the flakes missed by the top-feeders will sink into their territory, but make sure that they get their ration.

Never leave any food in the tank to go stale and rotten. If there are any flakes of food left uneaten within five minutes, skip the next feeding. You can feed your fish from two to four times a day.

Food from the pet shop

Aquarium fish have varied needs and some fishkeepers provide their food in the form of flakes. Tropical fish flakes contain a variety of foods. These include fish, meat, shrimp, flour, egg, cereals and other important foods. The recipes contain flakes suitable for a wide range of tropical fish species. There are flakes made up to different recipes for coldwater and marine fish. You should read the label on the food package carefully so that you do not, for instance, offer goldfish food to tropicals, or marine fish food to goldfish and other freshwater fish.

▼ **You can tell what level your fish feed at by studying their mouths.**

surface-feeder

mid-water feeders

bottom-feeders

◄ Feed goldfish little and often, two to four times a day. Healthy fish should rise eagerly for their food. If they fail to do so, you may be overfeeding them.

For larger fish, you can buy sticks, tablets or pellets made up to the correct recipes. These can be fed to the fish either whole, or broken up into smaller pieces according to the size of the mouths of your fish.

Fresh food

You may decide to feed your fish with fresh food now and again. As a change, they will enjoy live daphnia, water fleas and tubifex worms. Most pet shops that sell aquarium fish stock such foods.

You can also buy a food block or an automatic feeder for when you go on vacation. But the best thing is to get a friend to come in and check your fish every few days.

▼ In the community tank, fish may feed at all levels, some at the surface, some at mid-water and some on the bottom of the tank. The pet shop, or another aquarist, will advise you how to make sure that all your fish will receive the right kind of food.

Health and hygiene

Fish, like all pets, should be well cared for by their owners. Your fish should stay healthy if you give them a healthy environment and keep it so. Their well being depends on this, and on being properly fed but not overfed.

You should also make sure that you have a mixture of species that will get on well together. Avoid overcrowding. Remember, you can have about "one inch of fish" for each gallon of water. (See page 23.) And remember also that fish grow in size.

Care of the tank

At least once a month unplug the heater and remove a quarter of the water. Use a pad of absorbant cotton to remove algae from the front glass. Refill with water of the same temperature and quality. You should check the water temperature in the tropical tank

◄ ▲ This boy is siphoning water from his tank. First, he fills the tubing with water by submerging it completely. Then he pinches one end and brings it over the side of the tank so that it is lower than the other end and the water flows into the bucket. After removing a quarter of the water this way, he can refill the tank with clean water.

► The two most common fish diseases are Fin-rot (left) and "Ick" (White Spot) (right). It is easy to see when your fish has one of these diseases. You should ask your pet shop for advice.

each time you feed your fish. Also, count your fish in case one has died or been eaten. Never tap on the glass or make sudden movements to disturb the fish. Once a week, you should remove dead leaves from your plants and thin out the floating plants. Every two weeks or so, the filter should be removed and cleaned — how often depends on what kind of filter you have. Ask at your pet show how to maintain your filter.

Signs of illness

If you see fish gasping at the surface of your tank you will know that something is wrong. Your tank may be overcrowded, in which case you need more aeration, fewer fish or an extra tank; or the water may be **polluted** and a partial water change may be necessary.

The two most common fish diseases are Fin-rot and White Spot (usually called "Ick"). White Spot, a parasite, is seen as tiny white spots on the body. This disease is very contagious, and the whole tank should be treated, since the floor of the tank and the water also become infected.

If a fish appears unwell, you should seek advice from the pet shop. Both Ick and White Spot can be cured with chemicals sold there.

▲ Watch your fish every day for signs of ill health. If you see a fish gasping for breath near the surface, it means there is something wrong. Either the water is polluted, or the tank is overcrowded.

Breeding fish

It is natural for all animals to breed, and fish are no exception. When they are old enough to breed, fish reproduce by laying eggs or by giving birth to live young. The eggs are made fertile by the male either outside or inside the female's body. The way fish breed varies from one species to another.

When you stock your tank you should make sure that you know the breeding habits of each of your species. Breeding fish are divided into two groups, livebearers and egglayers.

◄ **In the top left-hand corner of this picture you can see a breeding trap for livebearers. After birth, the young fry escape through small holes in the trap, and so avoid being eaten by their mother.**

Livebearing fish

Livebearers do not lay eggs. Baby fish are formed inside the body of the female and are born live. The tiny fish may appear in batches of two or three at a time, and may total 100. Guppies, Mollies, Platies and Swordtails are all livebearers. They breed well in the aquarium, but you must watch out. Swordtails, and others too, are greedy fish and often eat their young.

▲ Siamese Fighting fish are bubble nest builders. The male builds the nest, and this consists of a mass of bubbles among water plants at the surface of the water. The bubbles support the hundreds of eggs laid by the female, and these are guarded by the male.

Some fishkeepers put expectant females inside a breeding trap in the tank. This is a small plastic container. It is made so that the young fry can escape through slits and avoid being eaten by the mother.

Egglaying fish

The egglayers are more difficult to breed from, and you would need a separate tank. There are bubble nest builders whose nests are made of air trapped in slime at the water's surface. This is often kept in place by plants. There are egg buriers, like some Killifish, which in the wild bury their eggs at the bottoms of shallow pools. When the pools dry up the eggs are protected by mud and hatch when the next rains come.

Among the strangest of all are the Cichlid mouth-brooders. As soon as she has laid her eggs, the female scoops them up into her mouth. She starves until the young fry hatch out and go hunting for food. Even then, they may come darting back to her mouth at the first sign of danger! She guards her young until they are able to fend for themselves.

Breeding tips — Egglaying fish	
Egglayers include Goldfish, Barbs, Danios, Tetras and Angelfish	
Egg scatterers	Before the fish spawn, cover the floor of the tank with small pebbles. The eggs will fall down the sides of the pebbles where hungry fish cannot reach them
Egg depositors	A small flower pot turned on its side will make a good place for the female to lay her eggs. You can arrange rocks to make suitable caves
Bubble nest builders	An aquarium top is helpful; so are floating plants
Egg buriers	You should cover the base of your tank with a layer of peat for the eggs to be buried in
Mouth-brooders	No special breeding quarters necessary

Keeping marine fish

So far we have only dealt with the fish that live in freshwater rivers and lakes. Keeping marine fish, that is to say the fish that live in the salt water of seas and oceans, is not for the beginner. But it may be something to look forward to when you have become an expert with freshwater fish.

Water is the most important part of a fish's environment. The saltiness of the water has to be the same in the marine tank as it is in the sea. The salts in the water are a mixture of many chemicals. They are dissolved in the water. If you put a spoonful of table salt in a glass of water and stir it, the salt dissolves and mixes with the tapwater. But the marine aquarist has to use special marine salt with tapwater to make seawater. The salts eat into metal, so marine tanks cannot have any metal parts. A part of the water has to be replaced each month.

Here are some of the beautiful marine fish which, some day, you might decide to keep as a marine aquarist.

▼ Many marine fish are extremely colorful, the Powder-blue Surgeon Fish (bottom) grows to 30 cm (12 in) in length. The red fish to the right is a Black-backed Anemone Fish. Farther to the right is a Flag-tail Surgeon Fish.

◄ The Yellow-tailed Anemone Fish lives with the sea anemone. These fish are also called Clownfish. By living close together the fish and the anemone give each other protection.

The Clownfish —size about 12 cm (4.72 in)

This beautiful fish lives close to sea anemones. When danger threatens, it takes refuge in the **tentacles** of the anemone. Its bright colors are a warning signal to keep away — the Clownfish and the anemone protect each other.

The Archer Fish —size about 24 cm (9.44 in)

The Archer Fish is not a marine fish but lives in coastal waters that are partly salt. This fish obtains its food by using water as a weapon. It squirts a jet from its mouth to knock insects off the branches of overhanging trees.

The Butterfly Fish —size about 20 cm (7.87 in)

There are a number of varieties. The "Four eye" species has an imitation eye on the body. It is a decoy to protect its real eyes from enemies. The Bennett's Butterfly Fish, which is yellow, also has this false eye.

The Mandarin Fish —size about 10 cm (3.93 in)

This beautiful fish is prized by aquarists. It has blue, green and orange patches with dark borders. The Mandarin Fish likes to hide at the bottom of the tank, under coral.

▼ The Archer Fish is not a marine fish, but lives in river mouths near the ocean. It is here seen squirting a jet of water to knock an insect off the branch of a tree.

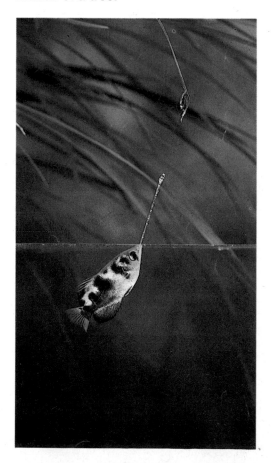

Seahorses

Perhaps one of the most fascinating animals that anyone could keep in the home is the seahorse. If some day you become a marine aquarist, you will want to try your luck with some varieties of seahorses. There are many different types and most of them live in tropical waters. The dwarfs, which measure about 5 cm (2 in), do well in marine tanks.

About seahorses

The seahorse does not look like a normal fish. It has very small side fins, and drifts along very slowly in an upright position. Seahorses need seaweed or coral around which to wrap their long tails while resting.

They feed on tiny marine animals, small fish and shrimp. Giving them the right environment and food, without which they soon become exhausted and die, is important.

▶ Seahorses have an unusual way of breeding. The female lays her eggs in a pouch on the belly of the male. He then cares for them until they hatch out as tiny seahorses. They grow rapidly and soon need a large amount of food.

▼ Seahorses are poor swimmers and use their tails for support. These Sri Lankan seahorses are using a Slate Pencil Urchin as an anchor. Seahorses and urchins are both slow movers and need armor for their protection.

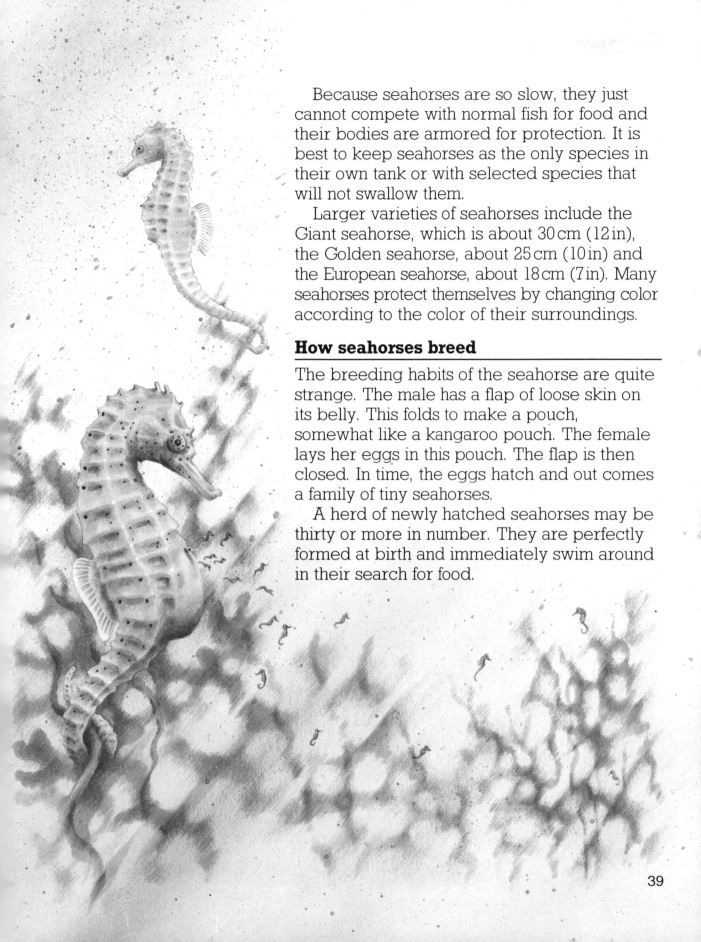

Because seahorses are so slow, they just cannot compete with normal fish for food and their bodies are armored for protection. It is best to keep seahorses as the only species in their own tank or with selected species that will not swallow them.

Larger varieties of seahorses include the Giant seahorse, which is about 30 cm (12 in), the Golden seahorse, about 25 cm (10 in) and the European seahorse, about 18 cm (7 in). Many seahorses protect themselves by changing color according to the color of their surroundings.

How seahorses breed

The breeding habits of the seahorse are quite strange. The male has a flap of loose skin on its belly. This folds to make a pouch, somewhat like a kangaroo pouch. The female lays her eggs in this pouch. The flap is then closed. In time, the eggs hatch and out comes a family of tiny seahorses.

A herd of newly hatched seahorses may be thirty or more in number. They are perfectly formed at birth and immediately swim around in their search for food.

Other marine animals

Fish are not the only beautiful animals that live in the sea. Sea anemones, corals and jelly fishes are all living animals. These are called **invertebrates**, that is to say animals without backbones. Most fish are vertebrates — they have backbones. Some invertebrates can be kept in a marine tank.

Many marine aquarists who live near the coast enjoy collecting some of these invertebrates. With care, they will survive in the marine tank among the fish, providing color and variety to the tank and adding to the interest for the hobbyist.

Anemones

Sea anemones reach their greatest size in very warm parts of the world. However, there are many beautiful species to be found in rock pools and caves around the coasts of Europe and the United States. They all have tentacles surrounding their mouths. They use these to capture and poison their prey. Small anemones can sometimes be found buried in the sand with only their tentacles showing. Or they may be attached to rocks.

▼ Corals are tiny animals that live very close together. The chalky tubes in which they live form clusters of different colors and shapes. Some look like trees, some are fan-shaped and others are ball-shaped. They make a colorful addition to the marine tank.

▲ Some people collect Fan Worms or Tube Worms in a marine aquarium. These stange creatures exist in long tubes fixed to the seabed. At one end of their bodies they throw out colorful tentacles in the shape of a fan. This is the "mouth" through which they feed on tiny animals called plankton.

Corals

Coral reefs are made up of millions and millions of corals of different shapes and colors. The living corals of the reef grow on top of millions of dead ones.

Corals, though somewhat like small sea anemones, live in hard tubes made of a kind of chalk. Coral reefs swarm with life, and under the water the forest of colorful corals becomes the home and territory of many fish both large and small.

For the aquarist, corals will make a natural environment for fish in the aquarium. Live or treated corals make good decoration in the tank, and varieties like the Sea Fan can be bought in some pet shops.

Sponges

Even sponges are sea animals! A sponge is full of holes, some of them small and some of them large. The sponge takes in seawater through the smaller holes. It soaks up food from the water. Then the water goes out through the larger holes. It is possible for a sponge to survive in the filtered water of an aquarium.

Showing your fish

When you become really interested in your hobby, you will want all the fish in your collection to be of the highest standard. Being your own judge is not easy unless you can compare your fish with those owned by others.

The first step is to join an aquarium society. Your local pet shop will be able to advise whether there is a club near your home. There may even be one that specializes in your favorite variety. These clubs have regular meetings, with talks by experts who like to help beginners. Many of the clubs hold film shows and competitions, as well as their own fish shows. Club members often travel to fish shows in other areas too.

Showing aquarium fish

Each animal put on show, whether it is a dog, cat, small caged pet, or even a fish, has what is known as a **standard** laid down for its variety. This is a standard of excellence that all owners try to achieve. For instance, marks will be given for color, size, fitness and so on. You will be able to get the standard for your chosen fish variety from your local club.

◀ If your fish have reached a high enough standard, you may wish to enter a pair for a local competition. You have to take them to the exhibition hall in a show tank. This tank must be small and light enough to be easily carried. It should not contain plants or decoration.

▲ Fish are divided into various classes or categories. A label giving the number of your class and your entry number, but not your name, is stuck on the side of your tank. There is a standard for each, such as ideal length and color. The judge has to pick out the winner of each class.

Fish are sometimes shown in pairs, usually in clear-sided tanks without decoration. There are also classes for decorated tanks. Often there is so little to choose between the pairs that the judge has a hard task in picking the winning fish. The first prize is given to the fish that is nearest to the standard laid down for that type of fish.

How to get started

Before showing your own fish you should go to as many fish shows as you can. There you may be able to talk to the exhibitors, and learn from them.

The show fish, like the show dog, has to be prepared for showing. First of all, the owner must feed the fish on good food to get it into the peak of condition. Only then will the coloring, state of the fins, and general fitness reach the standard. Also, the owner must prepare the fish for crowds and movement by putting the tank in a place in the home where people are always passing.

► This picture shows a winning pair of Armored Catfish in their show tank. They have been chosen by the judge as champions of their class. These fish have been judged for all the points in the standard. These include fitness, length, size, position of fins and barbels, and color.

Glossary

air pump: an electric pump that forces air down a tube into the tank. It creates bubbles and makes the water move around. It can operate some kinds of filters.

algae: very small, simple plants without roots, stems or leaves that grow on the glass and plant leaves.

aquarist: a person who keeps fish in an aquarium. A fishkeeper.

aquatic: growing or living in the water.

astrology: the study of the supposed influence of the stars on human affairs.

barbel: a beard-like whisker at the mouth of a fish, used as a feeler. There is also a European fish called a barbel.

carbon dioxide: a gas that is part of air. All animals, including fish, breathe it out. Plants take it in and use it to make food.

carnivorous: flesh-eating.

caudal: having to do with the tail.

community: a group of animals living together. A community tank is one in which different species of fish, if carefully selected, can live together peacefully.

dorsal: near or attached to the back. Dorsal fins are attached to the back of a fish.

environment: the surroundings in which animals and plants live. Fish are affected by the whole environment in which they live.

evaporation: the changing of a liquid into a vapor as a result of heat.

evolution: the way in which plants and animals have changed gradually over millions of years.

filter: an electric device that cleans the water in the tank. The water is pumped through the filter again and again, and the filter removes all the tiny pieces of solid matter from the water.

fin: a movable, flat part of a fish that sticks out from the body. Fish use fins for swimming and balancing in water.

fry: a very young fish.

gill: a part of the body of a fish used for breathing under water. Most animals with gills are unable to breathe out of water.

invertebrate: an animal without a backbone.

lateral line: a line of pores lying along both sides of the body of a fish. Beneath the line there are nerves that sense changes in water pressure and help the fish to avoid objects.

mammal: an animal with a warm body. Mammals give birth to live young that feed on their mother's milk.

ovoid: egg-shaped or oval.

oxygen: a gas found in air and in water. Animals need oxygen in order to survive.

pectoral: of or attached to the chest. Pectoral fins are attached to the sides of the body of many fish.

pollute: to spoil or poison the land or water.

scale: one of the small thin plates that cover the bodies of many fishes.

species: a particular kind of animal. Members of one species cannot usually breed with members of another species.

standard: written rules of excellence for each species of fish, by which one fish can be judged against another at a fish show.

tentacle: a long arm or feeler of a sea animal, used for feeling, eating, holding or stinging.

thermostat: a device that controls temperature.

tropics: the part of the earth that is close to the equator. The tropics are the hottest parts of the earth.

ventral: having to do with or attached to the belly. Ventral fins are attached to the belly of a fish.

vertebrate: an animal with a backbone.

Further reading

Aquarium Fish From Around the World by Klaus Payson. Lerner, 1970.
Aquarium Fish Survival Manual by Brian Ward. Baron, 1985.
The Language of Goldfish by Zibby Oneal. Viking, 1980.
Saltwater Tropical Fish in Your Home by Gail Campbell. Sterling, 1976.
Science-Hobby Book of Aquariums by Miriam Gilbert. Lerner, 1968.
Tropical Saltwater Aquariums: How to Set Them Up & Keep Them Going by Seymour Simon. Viking, 1976.
You and Your Pet: Aquarium Pets by Phil Steinberg. Lerner, 1978.

Aquarium magazines

Tropical Fish Hobbyist, T.F.H. Publications

Useful addresses

T.F.H. Publications, 211 W. Sylvania Avenue, Neptune, New Jersey 07753

Index